HOW SHOULD WE DEVELOP BIBLICAL **FRIENDSHIP?**

JOEL R. BEEKE
AND
MICHAEL A. G. HAYKIN

GW00585030

REFORMATION HERITAGE BOOKS
GRAND RAPIDS, MICHIGAN

How Should We Develop Biblical Friendship?
© 2015 by Joel R. Beeke and Michael A. G. Haykin

Reformation Heritage Books
2965 Leonard St. NE
Grand Rapids, MI 49525
616-977-0889 / Fax 616-285-3246
orders@heritagebooks.org
www.heritagebooks.org

Printed in the United States of America
18 19 20 21 22 23/10 9 8 7 6 5 4 3 2

ISBN 978-1-60178-381-3

For additional Reformed literature, request a free book list from Reformation Heritage Books at the above regular or e-mail address.

HOW SHOULD WE DEVELOP
BIBLICAL FRIENDSHIP?

*Ointment and perfume rejoice the heart: so doth the
sweetness of a man's friend by hearty counsel.*

—PROVERBS 27:9

Today's culture does not provide great encouragement for the nurture and development of deep,
long-lasting, satisfying friendships. Such friendships
take time and sacrifice. Early twenty-first-century
Western culture emphasizes extreme busyness and,
as a rule, promotes receiving and possessing more
than sacrificing and giving.[1] What is especially dis-
turbing is that the values of Western Christianity
often appear to be similar to those of the surround-
ing culture. As C. S. Lewis noted in his *Screwtape
Letters*, an ingenious commentary on spiritual war-
fare from the viewpoint of the devil, "In modern
Christian writings," there are "few of the old warn-
ings about Worldly Vanities, the Choice of Friends,

---

1. Diogenes Allen, *Love: Christian Romance, Marriage, Friendship*
(Cambridge, Mass.: Cowley Publications, 1987), 45–46.

and the Value of Time."[2] He is undoubtedly correct when it comes to the topic of friendship. Up until the last decade or so, books on Christian friendship were few and far between. Thankfully, this is beginning to change. Change it must, for friendship is one of the primary means God uses to strengthen His people. If our generation of believers gives little thought to this marvelous vehicle of divine grace, we will be the poorer for it. In what follows, then, we will explore what the Bible and some of our Christian forebears have said regarding friendship and then look at the way the rich experience of friendship in the past can be recaptured today.

In the ancient world, friendship was deemed to be of such vital importance that the Greek philosopher Plato (c. 428–c. 348 BC) devoted an entire book, the *Lysis*, as well as substantial portions of two other books, the *Phaedrus* and the *Symposium*, to a treatment of its nature. Aristotle (384–322 BC), the other leading thinker of the classical Greek period, also considered the topic of friendship significant enough that two of the ten books of the *Nicomachean Ethics*, his major work on ethical issues, discuss it. For the ancient Greeks—and the ancient Romans—friendship stood as one of the highest ideals of human life.

---

2. C. S. Lewis, *The Screwtape Letters*, in *The Best of C. S. Lewis* (Washington, D.C.: Canon Press, 1969), 43.

FRIENDSHIP IN THE HOLY SCRIPTURES

While we do not find such extended discussions of friendship in the Scriptures, the Bible speaks more about friendship than is often realized. Supreme friendship is reflected in God Himself, in the amazing love that exists between the three persons of the Trinity. The apostle John expresses the love of the Father and the Son for each other seventeen times (e.g., John 3:35). That covenantal love within the Godhead from eternity expresses itself in God's covenantal love to His people in time through the gospel. Because of that covenantal love, God could call Abraham His friend (Isa. 41:8). God's covenantal love to His unworthy people reflects an amazing depth when Jesus prays to His Father in John 17:23 "that the world may know that thou hast sent me, and hast loved them, as thou hast loved me."

Scripture also gives marvelous illustrations of what friendship should be. There is the covenantal friendship of David and Jonathan, for instance, a good example of "a friend that sticketh closer than a brother" (Prov. 18:24). Or that of Ruth and her mother-in-law, Naomi, proof that "a friend loveth at all times" (Prov. 17:17). Indeed, throughout Proverbs, that compendium on how to live wisely in this world, there are nuggets of advice about having friends and keeping them.[3] These texts leave the impression that

---

3. For some of these texts, see Proverbs 6:1–3; 16:28; 17:9, 17; 18:24; 27:6, 9–10, 14, 17. Also note the short meditation on friendship in Ecclesiastes 4:9–12.

the world of the Bible regarded friendship as an important part of life.

Two central ideas are found in the biblical representation of friendship.[4] The first is that friendship involves *mutual love* and *the knitting together of souls*. Deuteronomy provides the earliest mention of this when it describes a "friend, which is as thine own soul" (Deut. 13:6; cf. Lev. 19:18); that is, a friend is a companion of one's innermost thoughts and feelings. In 1 Samuel 18:1, we learn that "the soul of Jonathan was knit with the soul of David, and Jonathan loved him as his own soul." Here we see that the privileges and responsibilities of biblical friendship are rooted in mutual covenantal love, intercommunion, and personal investment in another.

The second metaphor that the Bible uses to represent friendship is the *face-to-face encounter*. In the tabernacle God spoke to Moses "face to face, as a man speaketh unto his friend" (Ex. 33:11; see also Num. 12:8). The image of a face-to-face encounter implies contact, communion, and a sharing of confidences, resulting in a melding together of minds, goals, and direction. One of the benefits of such face-to-face encounters between friends is the mutual uplift and encouragement that such encounters produce. As Proverbs 27:17 famously puts it: "Iron sharpeneth iron; so a man sharpeneth the countenance of his friend."

---

4. *Dictionary of Biblical Imagery*, ed. Leland Ryken et al. (Downers Grove, Ill.: InterVarsity Press, 1998), s.v. "friendship."

Paul's Understanding of Friendship

One of the most instructive examples of friendship in the Bible is that of Paul and Timothy. A common stereotype about Paul is that he was a sort of "Lone Ranger" evangelist, one who preferred to work by himself. In fact, in the New Testament narrative about his life and ministry, Paul is rarely found without friends and companions. He "delighted in the company of his fellows."[5] And of his companions, the dearest appears to have been Timothy. Though he was probably around twenty years Paul's junior, Timothy became the apostle's closest friend. In the words of the Bible scholar F. F. Bruce, Timothy "readily surrendered whatever personal ambitions he might have cherished in order to play the part of a son to Paul and help him in his missionary activity, showing a selfless concern for others that matched the apostle's own eagerness to spend and be spent for them."[6]

Timothy had joined Paul early on in the apostle's second missionary journey, that is, around AD 48 or 49 (Acts 16:1–3). As Timothy traveled with Paul, he saw firsthand what Paul described many years later as his "doctrine, manner of life, purpose, faith, long-suffering, charity, patience, persecutions, afflictions" (2 Tim. 3:10–11). This catalog from 2 Timothy is an excellent framework in which to observe details of

5. F. F. Bruce, *Paul: Apostle of the Heart Set Free* (Grand Rapids: Eerdmans, 1977), 457.

6. Bruce, *Paul*, 457.

these two men's friendship. First, Paul imparted to Timothy the doctrines of the Christian faith. Timothy grew to know the details of Paul's theology and doctrinal convictions. He learned that at the heart of all genuinely Christian theology is the triune God: God the Father, the Lord Jesus Christ, and the Holy Spirit. He came to be grounded in the fact that the gospel is centered on the death and resurrection of Christ, as the only way that men and women can come into a saving relationship with the one true and living God.

Then, Timothy also saw the way that Paul lived, his "manner of life," how he made decisions and determined the best use of his time. This manner of life dovetailed with Paul's "purpose" for living, namely, to glorify God and His Son, Christ Jesus. Timothy also witnessed Paul's "faith [and] long-suffering" as well as his "charity," his love for the people of God and compassion for those who were held in the darkness of sin. And Timothy saw the way that Paul responded with "patience" and perseverance to difficulties and that the apostle did not waver in his commitment to Christ despite "persecution [and] afflictions."

As Paul and Timothy spent this large amount of time together, Timothy's soul began to mirror Paul's, and his mind became increasingly attuned to the wavelengths of the apostle's thinking. Thus, Timothy's friendship with Paul was a means by which God sanctified the younger man, giving him an ever-increasing richness of thought about God and the gospel and an ever-growing desire for holiness and conformity to Christ. In 1 Corinthians 15:33 Paul urges the Corinthians to recognize that "evil communications corrupt good manners," that is to say, indulgence in bad company and evil companions has a destructive effect on the development of a life of goodness and virtue. Intimate friendships with evil men will invariably have a negative effect on our lives. If this is true from a negative standpoint, one can also say that good company promotes good habits. This was the effect that Paul undoubtedly had on Timothy. This was the effect that friendship with the eighteenth-century Baptist, Samuel Pearce (1766–1799), a man of great personal holiness, had on the Congregationalist William Jay (1769–1853). Jay, who had an influential ministry in Bath, England, for the first half of the nineteenth century, made this comment about the last time he saw Pearce alive: "What a savour does communion with such a man leave upon the spirit."[7] As Maurice Roberts said, "Our best friends are those whose company most makes us afraid to sin."[8]

---

7. *The Autobiography of William Jay*, ed. George Redford and John Angell James (1854 ed.; repr., Edinburgh: Banner of Truth, 1974), 372–73. For help in this and the previous paragraph, we are indebted to Maurice Roberts, "Christian Friendships," in his *The Thought of God* (Edinburgh: Banner of Truth, 1993), 175–76.

8. Roberts, "Christian Friendships," in *Thought of God*, 176.

Paul's Friendship with Timothy

The text in which the dearness of Paul's friendship with Timothy comes out most clearly is Philippians 2:19–22. The Philippian church had been evidently experiencing some measure of discord. Paul mentions it explicitly in chapter 4 when he urges Euodia and Syntyche to "be of the same mind in the Lord" (v. 2). In chapter 2 Paul urges the Philippians to be "likeminded"—the same phrase that Paul employs in Philippians 4:2—"having the same love, being of one accord, of one mind," looking out for not only their own interests but also those of others (vv. 2–4). To illustrate this admonition and make it clearly understood, Paul encourages the Philippians to meditate on the example of Christ, whose mind and heart were focused not on His own personal interests but on those of fallen humanity. So taken up was Christ with the lot of sinners that though He was fully God He "made himself of no reputation." He became incarnate and took upon Himself the burden of human sin and was "obedient unto death, even the death of the cross" (Phil. 2:6–8).

In Philippians 2:19–22 Paul gives a second example of being likeminded and having the interests of others at heart. This time he mentions his friend Timothy and says:

> I trust in the Lord Jesus to send Timotheus shortly unto you, that I also may be of good comfort, when I know your state. For I have no man likeminded, who will naturally care for your state.

> For all seek their own, not the things which are
> Jesus Christ's. But ye know the proof of him, that,
> as a son with the father, he hath served with me
> in the gospel.

From the words that Paul uses here it is clear that
he is commending Timothy as an example of Christ-
likeness. Timothy sincerely cares for the state of the
Philippians. He is genuinely concerned about their
needs as fellow believers and is not seeking to pro-
mote his own interests. And, as such, he displays
the mind of Christ. Paul can thus describe him in
verse 20 as "likeminded." Because of his desire to
be like Christ, Timothy fully shares Paul's heart and
mind and is thus a completely trustworthy agent and
representative of Paul.[9] Due to their age difference,
Paul refers to Timothy as his son when he goes on
to write that Timothy has proven his worth during
his ministry with Paul "as a son with his father." Paul
is always very careful to avoid giving the impression
that he is lord and master over the faith of others.
Timothy did not serve him, but together before God
they served the Lord of the gospel, Christ Jesus. We
see that Paul prizes his friendship with Timothy, and
we understand that it is based on a harmony of heart
and mind. Without such harmony there can be no
intimate friendship.

---

9. Panayotis Christou, "ΙΣΟΨΥΧΟΣ, Phil. 2:20," *The Journal of
Biblical Literature* 70 (1951): 293–96.

Paul's Hunger for Companionship while Facing Death
The final record of this friendship is found in 2 Timothy. This letter was written shortly before Paul's death at the hands of a Roman executioner. Paul wrote from a prison in Rome while Timothy was in Ephesus, on the coast of modern Turkey. Paul opens the letter by describing Timothy as a "beloved son" whom he regularly remembers in prayer and whom he eagerly desires to see. As he thinks of Timothy, he especially recalls the last time that the two were together, when Timothy broke down and wept (2 Tim. 1:2–4). This occasion may well have been when Paul was arrested.

After encouraging Timothy to hold fast to the gospel, to pursue godliness, and to fulfill his ministry, Paul tells his friend of his impending death. He faces this prospect of death with confidence, aware that he is saved and stands in a right relationship with "the Lord, the righteous judge" (2 Tim. 1:9; 4:6–8). But so strong is his friendship with Timothy that when he mentions his death, he urges his close friend to "do thy diligence to come shortly unto me" (2 Tim. 4:9). As he draws the letter to a close, he again urges his friend: "Do thy diligence to come before winter" (2 Tim. 4:21). During the winter months from November to March, it was dangerous to sail the Mediterranean, and much of the shipping in that region halted for that reason. Aware of this and conscious that his death was close, Paul urges Timothy to sail from Ephesus for Rome before the winter months. If not, then he would probably have to travel overland to Rome, which would take considerably longer and he might arrive too late.

Paul's longing to see his friend does not mean that he feared somehow that his friendship with Timothy would not be renewed in heaven. He would certainly have agreed with an observation made by Esther Edwards Burr (1732–1758), daughter of Jonathan Edwards (1703–1758): "True friendship is first enkindled by a spark from heaven, and heaven will never suffer it to go out, but it will burn to all eternity."[10]

FRIENDSHIP IN THE CHRISTIAN TRADITION

The spread of the church throughout the Roman Empire in the centuries immediately after the death and resurrection of Christ did not negate this rich appreciation of friendship in the biblical world. Alongside the Christian emphasis on showing love to all men and women—family, friends, acquaintances, even enemies—friendship continued to be highly valued. In fact, the emphasis placed on the unity in Christ of all Christians encouraged a high degree of spiritual intimacy that resembled, and even surpassed, the

---

10. *The Journal of Esther Edwards Burr 1754–1757*, ed. Carol F. Karlsen and Laurie Crumpacker (New York, N.Y.: Yale University Press, 1984), 92 (February 15, 1755). In this quote and subsequent quotes from Esther's journal, spelling and capitalization have been modernized.

intimacy that Graeco-Roman society deemed essential to the experience of genuine friendship.[11]

Gregory of Nazianzus (c. 329–389), a leading fourth-century theologian, could thus write of his friendship with Basil of Caesarea (c. 330–379) during their time together as students in Athens in the 350s:

> In studies, in lodgings, in discussions I had him as companion.... We had all things in common.... But above all it was God, of course, and a mutual desire for higher things, that drew us to each other. As a result we reached such a pitch of confidence that we revealed the depths of our hearts, becoming ever more united in our yearning.[12]

Given this estimation of friendship, it is no surprise that Gregory could also state, "If anyone were to ask me, 'What is the best thing in life?,' I would answer, 'Friends.'"[13]

In the Middle Ages, Aelred of Rievaulx (1110–1167) penned a classic on this subject, *Spiritual Friendship*. For Aelred, genuine friendship must "begin in Christ, continue in Christ, and be perfected in Christ." And such spiritual friendship is to be highly prized, for "in human affairs nothing more sacred is striven for, nothing more useful is sought after, nothing more

---

11. Carolinne White, *Christian Friendship in the Fourth Century* (Cambridge: Cambridge University Press, 1992), 57.

12. Gregory of Nazianzus, "On His Life," in *Three Poems*, trans. Denis Molaise Meehan, in The Fathers of the Church, vol. 75 (Washington, D.C.: The Catholic University of America Press, 1987), 83–84.

13. White, *Christian Friendship*, 70.

difficult is discovered, nothing more sweet experienced, and nothing more profitable possessed. For friendship bears fruit in this life and in the next."[14]

John Calvin's Friendships

At the beginning of the modern era, John Calvin (1509–1564) had a rich appreciation of friendship. The French Reformed historian Richard Stauffer reckoned that there were few men at the time of the Reformation "who developed as many friendships" as Calvin.[15] Calvin's love for and dependence on a number of close friends has been studied by Machiel A. van den Berg, a Dutch Reformed pastor, in the recent work *Friends of Calvin*.[16] Friends such as his ministerial coworkers, Guillaume Farel (1489–1565) and Pierre Viret (1511–1571), are familiar to those who have read about Calvin's life. Calvin's other friendships, such as with the Dutch couple Lord and Lady de Falais, are much less known. A close look at these friendships reveals how significant they were for the Protestant Reformation and for Calvin's personal spiritual maturity.

In his preface to his commentary on Titus, Calvin celebrates his friendship with Farel and Viret, and

---

14. Aelred of Rievaulx, *Spiritual Friendship*, trans. Mary Eugenia Laker (Kalamazoo, Mich.: Cistercian Publications, 1977), 53, 71.

15. Richard Stauffer, *The Humanness of John Calvin*, trans. George H. Shriver (Nashville: Abingdon Press, 1971), 47.

16. Machiel A. van den Berg, *Friends of Calvin*, trans. Reinder Bruinsma (Grand Rapids: Eerdmans, 2009).

we get a good sense of the importance of friendship for ministry:

> I do not believe that there have ever been such friends who have lived together in such a deep friendship in their everyday style of life in this world as we have in our ministry. I have served here in the office of pastor with you two. There was never any appearance of envy; it seems to me that you two and I were as one person.... And we have shown through visible witness and good authority before men that we have among us no other understanding or friendship than that which has been dedicated to the name of Christ, has been to the present time of profit to his church, and has no other purpose but that all may be one in him with us.[17]

The core of this brotherly friendship is seen best in the three men's correspondence. There are 163 extant letters from Calvin to Farel and 137 from Farel to Calvin, and there are 204 existing letters from Calvin to Viret and 185 from Viret to Calvin. In them there is not only frank discussion of theological and ecclesiastical matters but also an openness regarding the problems of their private lives. To note but one example, on January 27, 1552, Calvin wrote to Farel and chided him for reports that he had heard about the undue length of Farel's sermons. "You have frequently confessed," Calvin reminds his friend, "that you were aware of defect, and that you were

---

17. As quoted in Stauffer, *Humanness of John Calvin*, 57.

endeavouring to correct it." Calvin went on to urge
Farel to shorten his sermons lest Satan use Farel's
failing in this regard to destroy the many good
things being produced by his ministry.[18] This is iron
sharpening iron, as Proverbs 27:17 puts it, and a good
reminder that times of advance in church history
result when God works through bands of friends.

What gave these friendships a depth unmatched
by many friendships of our day was the conviction
that these relationships were wrought by God and
were eternal. As Calvin wrote to Philipp Melanchthon
(1497–1560), "The distance in place cannot prevent
us—content with the bond that Christ has established
through his blood and has enclosed in our hearts
through his Spirit—from holding on to the hope…
that we will in the end live together eternally and in
eternal enjoyment of our love and friendship."[19]

An Eighteenth-Century Friendship

The importance of friendship in the Christian life was
still an important subject in the eighteenth century.
Esther Edwards Burr, quoted above, unequivocally
declared: "Nothing is more refreshing to the soul
(except communication with God himself), than the
company and society of a friend."[20] The wife of a

18. Calvin to Farel, January 27, 1552, in John Calvin, *Tracts and
Letters*, ed. Jules Bonnet and trans. David Constable (1858 ed.; repr.,
Edinburgh: Banner of Truth, 2009), 5:337.

19. Van den Berg, *Friends of Calvin*, ix.

20. *Journal of Esther Edwards Burr*, 185 (January 23, 1756).

busy college president (Aaron Burr Sr. [1716–1757], second president of the College of New Jersey, later Princeton University), and the mother of two small children, Esther earnestly sought to know the presence of God in the hustle and bustle of her daily life. As she did so, she came to appreciate that friends are a divine gift. Writing in her diary on January 23, 1756, she says that she was convinced that it is "a great mercy that we have any friends—What would this world be without 'em—A person who looks upon himself to be friendless must of all creatures be miserable in this Life—'tis the life of life."[21] For Esther, Christian friends were one of this world's greatest sources of happiness. Why did she put such a value upon friendship? Surely because she knew that Christian friends and conversation with them is vital for spiritual growth.

Similar convictions are found in her writing the previous year on April 20, 1755, to a friend named Sarah Prince:

> I should highly value (as you my dear do) such charming friends as you have about you—friends that one might unbosom their whole soul to…. I esteem religious conversation one of the best helps to keep up religion in the soul, excepting secret devotion, I don't know but the very best— then what a lamentable thing that 'tis so neglected by God's own children.[22]

---

21. *Journal of Esther Edwards Burr*, 185.
22. *Journal of Esther Edwards Burr*, 112.

Notice the connection between friendship and what Esther calls "religious conversation." For the Christian, true friends are those with whom one can share the deepest things of life. They are people with whom one can be transparent and open. In Esther's words, they are people to whom one can "unbosom [one's] whole soul." And in conversation about spiritual things, the believer can find strength and encouragement for living the Christian life. In referring to conversation with friends as "one of the best helps to keep up religion in the soul," Esther viewed it as a means of grace, one of the ways that God the Holy Spirit keeps Christians in fellowship with the Savior. As another New England Christian, Nathanael Emmons (1745–1840), put it in one of his favorite maxims: "A man is made by his friends."[23]

Two Baptist Friends

Another excellent example from the eighteenth century is the friendship of John Ryland Jr. (1753–1825) and Andrew Fuller (1754–1815). In 1793 Ryland was called to be the pastor of Broadmead Baptist Church in Bristol, England, as well as the principal of Bristol Baptist Academy. He stayed in these offices until his death in 1825.

---

23. As quoted in Edwards A. Park, "Memoir of Nathanael Emmons," in *The Works of Nathanael Emmons, D.D.*, ed. Jacob Ide (Boston: Congregational Board of Publication, 1861), 1:115.

Among Ryland's lifelong friends—indeed, his closest friend—was Andrew Fuller, pastor of Kettering Baptist Church, Northamptonshire, from 1782 to 1815. Fuller was a prolific writer of theological works and so influential a theologian that one author not long after his death described him as the "elephant of Kettering." He was also secretary of the Baptist Missionary Society, founded in 1792. Ryland and Fuller first met in 1778 when both were in their midtwenties and were rethinking a number of vital spiritual issues. It was not long before they were the closest of friends. Fuller's move to Kettering in 1782 meant that the two now had frequent opportunities to talk, pray, and spend time together, for Northampton and Kettering are only thirteen miles apart. What initially attracted Ryland and Fuller to each other was the discovery that they shared "a strong attachment to the same religious principles, a decided aversion to the same errors, a predilection for the same authors," in particular, the writings of Jonathan Edwards.[24] They had that fundamental aspect of a good friendship, a union of hearts, which we have seen is essential to the biblical understanding of friendship. Their friendship was unbroken for the next thirty-seven years, until Fuller died in 1815.

---

24. John Ryland Jr., *The Indwelling and Righteousness of Christ No Security against Corporal Death, but the Source of Spiritual and Eternal Life* (London: W. Button & Son, 1815), 35.

About a week before his death, Fuller made one last request of Ryland: Would he preach his funeral sermon? Ryland agreed, and toward the end of his sermon, he reminisced that their friendship had "never met with one minute's interruption, by one unkind word or thought, of which I have any knowledge," and that the wound caused by the loss of "this most faithful and judicious friend" was something that would never be healed in this life.[25] As a way of garnering financial support for Fuller's family, Ryland published a biography of his close friend in 1816, the year after Fuller's death. In the introduction he described his friendship with Fuller:

> Most of our common acquaintance are well aware, that I was his oldest and most intimate friend; and though my removal to Bristol, above twenty years ago, placed us at a distance from each other, yet a constant correspondence was all along maintained; and, to me at least, it seemed a tedious interval, if more than a fortnight elapsed without my receiving a letter from him.[26]

They kept their friendship alive and intact through the medium of the written letter. So it was that for more than twenty years the two men faithfully corresponded with one another. Both Ryland and Fuller knew well that friendship is a fragile treasure, one

---

25. Ryland Jr., *Indwelling and Righteousness of Christ*, 36–37.

26. John Ryland Jr., *The Work of Faith, the Labour of Love, and the Patience of Hope, Illustrated; in the Life and Death of the Rev. Andrew Fuller*, 2nd ed. (London: Button & Son, 1818), viii–ix.

that can be neglected or lost in the busyness of life if they did not give it the care and attention it needed. Haddon Robinson has rightly noted: "Even strong friendships require watering or they shrivel up and blow away."[27] If we are going to have friendships like that of Ryland and Fuller, we need to invest time and energy in them. How many of us have friendships that have died over the years simply because we have been too busy with other matters of life?

THE ART OF BUILDING GODLY FRIENDSHIPS

Given the great value of Christian friendships, what can you do to build them? If you are convinced that you need Christian friendship, then how do you find it and cultivate it? Most importantly, you must receive a new heart and live a daily life of faith and repentance in order to *build your friendship with God* through Jesus Christ as your covenant-establishing and covenant-keeping Redeemer. Jonathan Holmes writes, "Rather than serving as an end in itself, biblical friendship serves primarily to bring glory to Christ, who brought us into friendship with the Father. It is indispensable to the work of the gospel in the earth, and an essential element of what God created us for."[28] Therefore, use the means of grace,

27. Haddon Robinson, "Laughing the Night Away," *Christianity Today* 37, no. 3 (March 8, 1993): 15.

28. Jonathan Holmes, *The Company We Keep: In Search of Biblical Friendship* (Adelphi, Md.: Cruciform Press, 2014), 27. Thanks to Paul Smalley for his valuable assistance on this section.

such as Bible reading, meditation, and prayer, to grow in knowing your covenant-befriending God and to grow in your walk with Him. Use the public means of grace in the gatherings of the church. Learn to see your sins against God and your need for the Savior who died to pay the ransom price for sinners and rose again to give them eternal life. Seek grace from God to be experientially acquainted with a life of daily conversion so that you may grow in grace from the inside out. Live for the glory of God.

Christ taught us that loving our neighbors is the second greatest commandment; the first is loving the Lord with all our hearts (Matt. 22:37–39). Only when love for Christ rules your heart through the gospel will be you be prepared to love men, women, and children and thus be their authentic friend. Jesus enunciated a basic principle of friendship when He taught us to do unto others as we would have them do unto us (Matt. 7:12). Otherwise you will use people to get approval, control, self-righteousness, pleasure, prestige, or some other selfish end.[29]

In your friendships, let God alone be God. Do not turn friends into idols. If you begin to feel that you cannot live without a person, then you have forgotten that Christ is your life (Col. 3:4)—no one else. God alone has the right to be your ultimate

---

29. For a searching diagnostic of how we use friendships for sinful heart aims, see Amy Baker, *Getting to the Heart of Friendships* (Bemidji, Minn.: Focus Publishing, 2010).

source of wisdom, truth, right and wrong, faith and hope. Furthermore, remember that the development of friendships is not under your control, but under God's. Sometimes acquaintances who look promising never develop into deep friends. Friendship can be frustrating, and misplaced friendship can turn into disastrous betrayal. A new friendship may surprise you, or an old friend may be suddenly removed from your life. The point is that as you labor to be a friend to others, submit to God's providence. Jerry and Mary White wrote, "God does not intend that every friendship we attempt to initiate should develop."[30] As you strive to be a friend, you must recognize the mystery of how friendships come to pass. You cannot make someone be your faithful friend. God is Lord of friendship.

God works through means, however, and in the ordinary course of life we should take action to develop friendships with people around us. Christian friendship requires *discernment*. You cannot assume that everyone whom you find attractive or pleasant would make a good friend. Too often people make promises of friendship and success hoping that you will help them achieve their wicked goals, but they will lead you to your death (Prov. 1:10–19). There are people who will love you and stick with you, but others only want to get something from you

---

30. Jerry and Mary White, *Friends and Friendship: The Secrets of Drawing Closer* (Colorado Springs: NavPress, 1982), 56.

and will quickly desert you in hard times (Prov. 17:17; 19:4, 6–7). Consider how this person treats his family and other colleagues. Why would he treat you differently? Beware of friendships with someone given over to sin, such as anger, lest you become like him (Prov. 22:24–25). There are times when a culture is so degenerate and the godly so rare that you must carefully guard your heart, even among associates and family members (Mic. 7:5–6). The man or woman who fears the Lord, shows kindness to others, and diligently works in his or her daily calling is a friend worthy of your trust and admiration (Prov. 31:10–31). Choose wisely whom you let into your life and heart.

One aspect of discernment is recognizing that God gives us friends on different levels. Jesus, in His earthly ministry, related in different ways to the crowds who heard Him, the disciples who followed Him, the twelve apostles who were His daily companions, and Peter, James, and John as His closest friends. Think of the levels of friendship as concentric circles of mutual trust and knowledge. Outside the outermost circle are *strangers*, people you know little or nothing about. Level 1 consists of *acquaintances* whom you have met but may share little with. In level 2 are *allies* whom you have learned to trust with some things that are important to you as you work toward commonly held goals. Level 3 represents *companions* with whom you share significant aspects of your life and work. A step further in friendship is level 4, consisting of *confidants*—very

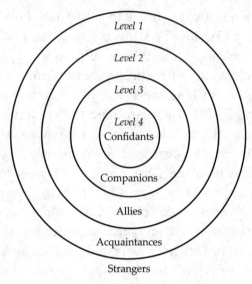

Figure 1: Circles of Friendship

close friends who are as one soul with you, with whom you share your deepest hopes and fears.

How would you use these circles to describe the different levels of your relationships? Don't assume that just because you go to church activities you have friends. Shawn McEvoy confesses, "I've been heavily involved in our Adult Bible Fellowship class at church for over five years now, and I can count on one hand the times I've done something outside of church with any of the men in that group."[31] As

---

31. Shawn McEvoy, "Men and Christian Friendship: It Won't Just Happen on Its Own," Crosswalk.com, April 15, 2008, http://www. crosswalk.com/faith/men/men-and-christian-friendship-it-wont-just-happen-on-its-own-11573347.html.

Holmes writes, to enter into biblical friendship, we need to go "beyond fellowship," at least insofar as Christians today commonly use the word *fellowship*.[32]

We should especially cultivate friendship in our families. If you are married, then you should work to make your spouse your closest confidant. However, it is possible to find deep friendships outside of marriage, such as the bond of brotherly love between David and Jonathan. We should realize, however, that level 4 friendships are very rare. God made us for such friendships in Paradise, but we forfeited them in the fall. We should be thankful to have one such friend and count ourselves greatly blessed if we have three to five in a lifetime.

To some extent, these levels oversimplify the complexity of our relationships, but they help us to recognize that there are different degrees of friendship, and it takes time and effort to move from one to another. People who try to leap from outside the circle to level 4 create unstable and sometimes dangerous relationships without a firm foundation of mutual knowledge, commitment, and trust. Such impatience and immaturity often leads to grievous sin and broken hearts.

Though we must be patient in developing Christian friendships, we must not be passive. Christians are called to do life together. Contrary to the individualism that is glorified in Western culture, we need to

32. Holmes, *Company We Keep*, 18.

realize that the Christian life has not been designed to be lived in solitude. Real Christianity is not a solitary life, but one lived in community. And friendships are to be a part of this experience of community.

PRACTICAL STEPS TOWARD DEEPENING FRIENDSHIP

When you find people with the potential for real Christian friendship, work at being a Christian friend to others and prayerfully seek God's blessing on developing relationships. Here are ten ways you can seek to cultivate Christian friendship. Think of them as pathways from outside the circle to level 4.

1. *Talk together.* Most friendships begin when one person starts talking to another person whom he does not know. Jerry and Mary White write, "New friendships demand a first move from someone. They don't erupt spontaneously, nor do they grow without words and communication. New friendships depend upon one person's willingness to step out and approach another."[33] Don't wait for someone else to talk to you. Go up to someone, ask a few questions, seek a common interest, get to know the person, and share a little about yourself.

If you feel shy around other people and find it hard to start conversations, remember what the Bible says is true about you. As the Whites have said, the

33. White, *Friends and Friendship,* 52.

Bible teaches that "God has lovingly created every person with valuable qualities—that includes you!" (Gen. 1:27), and, "We have a responsibility before God to extend our lives to others" (Eph. 2:10).[34] You have something to give to others and a stewardship from God to share it.

Build relationships through godly conversation. Don't talk about your life as if you were a practical atheist, but as you talk about life, constantly acknowledge the Lord of life. Sprinkle your conversations with the salty truth of Christ. And share with your closest friends your spiritual experiences, exercises, sorrows, and joys. Richard Baxter wrote, "The most necessary direction for a fruitful tongue is to get a well-furnished mind, and a holy heart, and to walk with God in holiness yourselves: for out of the abundance of the heart the mouth will speak."[35]

God is pleased with such spiritual fellowship and honors it. Malachi 3:16 says, "Then they that feared the LORD spake often one to another: and the LORD hearkened, and heard it, and a book of remembrance was written before him for them that feared the LORD, and that thought upon his name." In former centuries, God's children seemed to converse with each other deeply about spiritual truths and experiences much more frequently than they do

---

34. White, *Friends and Friendship*, 59.

35. Richard Baxter, *A Christian Directory*, in *The Practical Works of Richard Baxter* (1846; repr., Morgan, Pa.: Soli Deo Gloria, 1996), 1:817.

today. In the post-Reformation era small fellowship groups were common in the Netherlands, Scotland, England, Germany, and New England. Happily, in some circles they are springing up again today, but too many of God's people still don't have any friends to whom they may bare their souls in deep, spiritual conversation.

When such a friendship is developed, it becomes extraordinarily meaningful to both people. Then the two Christians can speak freely and naturally about matters both spiritual and natural, often moving from the spiritual to the natural and back to the spiritual with no awkwardness. Both feel that they benefit from this godly, real conversation with each other.

One of the great hindrances to godly conversation today is electronic media. Not only does this media shower us with unbelief and moral filth, but its pervasiveness kills relationships. Generations ago, families would sit and talk with each other. They often included friends at the table. On warm evenings, they might sit on the front porch and visit with anyone walking down their road. Today, families sit facing a large screen, paying little attention to each other but consuming hours of video entertainment derived from other people's lives (generally fictional). They may not even watch the same programs, for one person is watching a movie in a bedroom, another is playing a video game on a tablet in the den, a third is checking her Facebook on her smartphone, and the fourth is watching a sports event in the living room. Even at a restaurant, it is not unusual to find conversations interrupted by cell phone calls and text messages. As useful as computers and electronic media are for sharing information, if we are going to grow in friendship, we must have times when we turn off the media, look each other in the face, and talk.

2. *Listen together*. The best friends listen well. Most of us are eager to have the attention of others and be heard. James said, "Let every man be swift to hear, slow to speak, slow to wrath" (1:19). Juanita Ryan writes that silence is a "skill which is essential to listening." She explains,

> For most of us this is the most difficult of all the skills. We must be quiet. It seems quite simple. Unfortunately, our anxiety mounts where there are pauses which last for a few seconds.... What we fail to realize is that people need time and silence to think. They need to reflect and organize their thoughts and discover what they are feeling.[36]

Listening is not mere passive silence; we must be active listeners. We must pay attention to the person speaking with our eyes, ears, and mind. What is he communicating with his words, tone of voice, facial expressions, and body language? Too often our thoughts are a thousand miles away. We may assume that we already know what the person is

---

36. Juanita Ryan, *Standing By: Being There for a Friend in Crisis* (Wheaton, Ill.: Tyndale House, 1984), 80–81.

talking about and impatiently plan what we want to say while he is still talking. How arrogant we can be! When we listen, "in lowliness of mind let each esteem [the] other better than themselves" (Phil. 2:3). We can also ask good questions that encourage the person to open up further and help us to understand him or her better. Respond to your friend with a question that shows you are interested in drawing him or her to open up to you, much the way Jesus did with the two companions traveling to Emmaus (see Luke 24:17–19). Take a genuine interest in other people as God's children.

Listen for more than information. Listen to know a person. Try to understand his or her point of view. Open your heart and let your emotions answer your friend's. "Rejoice with them that do rejoice, and weep with them that weep" (Rom. 12:15). In so doing, you will become like Jesus Christ, the sympathetic High Priest who is "touched with the feeling of our infirmities," for He too is human and has suffered (Heb. 4:15).

A listening ear is critical to the nurture of the friendships that this booklet has been describing. Far too many Christians are shaped by the self-oriented culture of our day and are wrapped up in their own interests, plans, and ambitions and so have little time to listen, really listen, to others. The evidence is found in many people's inability to ask questions of one another (except when they are trying to get something out of each other). Frequently conversations are little better than two simultaneous monologues instead of a genuine exchange of ideas and thoughts prompted by asking questions. Here, too, our Lord sets the pattern. Was not His ministry filled with asking questions? Did He not have compassion on people, taking notice of their needs?

3. *Serve together.* Find ways to work side by side in God-honoring projects for the advancement of the kingdom of Christ. One of the best things that lonely Christians can do is to get involved in the ministries of the church. When Paul commended Timothy to the Philippian church, his words gave us a taste of the deep friendship they shared: "For all seek their own, not the things which are Jesus Christ's. But ye know the proof of him, that, as a son with the father, he hath served with me in the gospel" (Phil. 2:21–22). Serving Christ together bonds friends like family. Just as the heat of battle fuses individual soldiers into "a band of brothers," as Shakespeare once said,[37] so serving together in Christ's army makes a "fellow soldier" into "my brother" (Phil. 2:25).

Christian friendship carries an elevated nobility when it rises above merely personal aims and seeks the good of humanity and the glory of Christ. Holmes writes, "Biblical friendship exists when two or more people, bound together by a common faith in Jesus Christ, pursue him and his kingdom with

---

37. William Shakespeare, *Henry V*, act 4, scene 3.

intentionality and vulnerability."[38] Serving lifts our eyes from our natural selfishness, and in a common cause we come to know each other more deeply in both our strengths and weaknesses and to love each other with greater loyalty.

4. *Enjoy life together*. Friendship is more than a working partnership or a support system for the suffering. Friends multiply their joys by sharing them. One of the most basic ways is by eating together. Don't overspiritualize Christian friendship; two of its most important tools are a fork and a spoon (or chopsticks for some friends). As Christ's ministry shows, eating together communicates powerful messages of love and social acceptance. When we invite others into our homes for a meal, the acceptance, vulnerability, and self-disclosure of hospitality deepens the joy even further. Friends become as family.

A true friend is one with whom you can be playful and serious at the same time. The Bible teaches that God has appointed "a time to weep, and a time to laugh" (Eccl. 3:4). Do you recognize the times to have fun and make good use of them? Who do you enjoy being with the most? McEvoy writes that every March he spends a long weekend with about a dozen Christian men whom he has known since college. They go fishing, talk about their common interests, eat good food, and share what's going on

---

38. Holmes, *Company We Keep*, 27.

in their lives. Though they have been through great trials, they love God, and McEvoy writes, "I can't wait to get out of town to really bounce ideas and prayers off my friends, really seek out ways we can help each other, while at the same time destroying them by catching more fish."[39]

5. *Think together.* God calls us not only to be one in activity and one in feeling but also to be of one mind.[40] Discussing the truths of God is an important way that friends sharpen each other (Prov. 27:17). Hugh Black says, "There must be fellowship in the deepest things of the soul, community in the highest thoughts."[41] Talk about God, God's Word, and how God's glory appears in God's world. Help each other to love the Lord with all your minds.

Don't be afraid to debate ideas with brotherly and sisterly love. Have the humility to admit that you are often wrong and need to learn more, and have the courage to speak up for what you believe. Cultivate the kinds of friendships that allow you to disagree, learn from each other in the process, and end the conversation with mutual respect and affection.

Shallow conversations produce shallow minds. David Benner writes,

---

39. McEvoy, "Men and Christian Friendship."

40. Romans 15:5–6; 2 Corinthians 13:11; Philippians 1:27; 2:2; 1 Peter 3:8.

41. Hugh Black, *Friendship* (Guelph, Ont.: Joshua Press, 2008), 27.

> Friends who enjoy soul intimacy never settle for
> gossip or simple information exchange. Instead,
> they use the data of events as springboards for the
> sharing of feelings, perceptions, values, ideas, and
> opinions.... Most important, however, spiritual
> intimacy involves sharing our experience of God.[42]

6. *Be together*. Never underestimate the power of personal presence. When it comes to friendship, there is no substitute for time together. It certainly involves communication, but it aims for communion—sharing life together. Friendship has been defined as "the personal bond of a shared life."[43] Often friendships start because our families, jobs, or interests bring us together with someone on a regular basis. Yet rarely does life make friendship easy for long. If the friendship is to continue and grow, it will cost us something. Holmes says, "If we want biblical friendship, we must be willing to invest a resource that is limited and irreplaceable. We must invest our time."[44]

True friendships take time: it takes time to build into each other's lives. The transparency and trust essential to true friendship cannot be established overnight. Other things, lesser goods, need to be sacrificed to develop and maintain genuine friendships. Rather

---

42. David G. Benner, *Spiritual Companions: The Gift of Spiritual Friendship and Direction* (Downers Grove, Ill.: InterVarsity Press, 2002), 73–74.

43. Joel R. Beeke, *Friends and Lovers: Cultivating Companionship and Intimacy in Marriage* (Adelphi, Md.: Cruciform Press, 2012), 11.

44. Holmes, *Company We Keep*, 63.

than spending time indulging in the various forms of social media, it might be better to actually sit down with a friend and have a face-to-face conversation.

As a friendship grows, it focuses less on what we do and more on with whom we do it. We often think of friends as people with whom we like to do our favorite activities. They are our friends because we play games together, talk politics together, or go to the orchestra together. As we said earlier, there is a special pleasure in enjoying such events with friends. However, what if the joint events and activities had to cease? Would your friendship disappear? If so, how close a friendship was it? As one author writes, "The real test of friendship is: Can you literally do nothing with the other person? Can you enjoy together those moments of life that are utterly simple?"[45] When someone is your friend, you don't just get together for the sake of an activity that you enjoy. Your joy in the activity largely comes from doing it with that particular person because he is your friend. Your pleasure springs from loving your friend and enjoying God's glory with and through him.

In life's crises, the best gift of friendship is just being there. Hobbies, sports, and entertainment mean little at the graveside. When someone suffers profound loss, we sometimes are tempted to stay

---

45. Eugene Kennedy, as quoted in Ted W. Armstrong with Robert C. Larson, *The Fine Art of Friendship: Building and Maintaining Quality Relationships* (Nashville: Thomas Nelson, 1985), 18–19.

away because we don't know what to say. We forget that in the moment of greatest suffering people do not need words as much as companionship. One man recounts,

> I was sitting, torn by grief. Someone came and talked to me of God's dealings, of why it happened, of hope beyond the grave. He talked constantly, he said things I knew were true. I was unmoved, except to wish he'd go away. He finally did.
>
> Another came and sat beside me. He didn't talk. He didn't ask leading questions. He just sat beside me for an hour or more, listened when I said something, answered briefly, prayed simply, left. I was moved. I was comforted. I hated to see him go.[46]

Just as friendships are born by being together and live by investing time together, so they die from lack of time together. Maintaining a friendship requires regular contact. Though sometimes circumstances create that contact naturally, often we must exercise a discipline of seeking that person regularly. The easiest way to kill a friendship is by neglect. As the saying goes, out of sight is out of mind. A year without any personal contact cools what was once a vibrant relationship, and after several years the friendship is just history. We move on. If you want to keep a friendship alive, make an effort to regularly reach out to your friend through a visit, a letter, or a phone call.

---

46. Joe Bayly, as quoted in Ryan, *Standing By*, 61–62.

7. *Trust together*. Hugh Black writes, "Trust is the first requisite for making a friend. How can we be anything but alone, if our attitude toward men is one of armed neutrality, if we are suspicious...? Suspicion kills friendship."[47] Though the Bible warns us not to put our ultimate trust and hope in man, but in the Lord alone, it also speaks of a healthy measure of trust regarding people who prove themselves faithful by God's grace.[48] Proverbs 31:11 says of a virtuous woman that "the heart of her husband doth safely trust in her." We see this exemplified in a son's trust in his godly father, who appeals to him, "My son, give me thine heart, and let thine eyes observe my ways" (Prov. 23:26).

The Whites' definition of friendship highlights the importance of trust: "A friend is a trusted confidant to whom I am mutually drawn as a companion and an ally, whose love for me is not dependent on my performance, and whose influence draws me closer to God."[49] While we could not say that about every level of friendship, certainly it describes the small inner circle of friends we long to have.

Build trust gradually by proving yourself faithful and giving opportunities to your friend to prove himself faithful to you. That requires you to make yourself

---

47. Black, *Friendship*, 25.

48. Compare Jeremiah 17:5–8 with Romans 15:14; 2 Thessalonians 3:4; and 2 Timothy 2:2.

49. White, *Friends and Friendship*, 13.

vulnerable by revealing your weaknesses, needs, and flaws. Don't dump your life story on a new friend all at once, but take small steps over time. By developing a history of mutual faithfulness, you develop a foundation of trust on which to build for the future.

Don't be quick to jettison your trust in others once it is established. We should not be naïve, for people can deceive us and prove to be wicked hypocrites, but we also should not believe every rumor about a friend. Malicious and foolish gossip can poison a healthy friendship and separate the best of friends (Prov. 16:28; 17:9). As Ronald Reagan said, "Trust, but verify." Establish the truth about suspicions and accusations before allowing them to cast a shadow over your friend's character.

Learn to distinguish between betrayal and disappointment. If a friend disappoints you, it hurts, but it does not necessarily display a damning character flaw. It may be that he sincerely cares for you and generally walks in integrity, but he has stumbled. Experiences like that can teach us to rely on God more and to show more grace to others. Betrayal, on the other hand, shows a hypocritical heart and lack of integrity. While you should show mercy and seek reconciliation with someone who has betrayed you, your trust was violated and may take a long time to rebuild.

Beware of letting fear or cynicism keep you from ever trusting anyone. The walls you use to shut others out will not protect you, but will only imprison you. Black says, "Every relationship means risk, but we must take the risk; for while nearly all our sorrows come from our connection to others, nearly all our joys have the same source. We cannot help ourselves; for it is part of the great discipline of life."[50] Learn from your mistakes, grow in discernment, and move ahead in building new relationships.

8. *Pray together*. When we worship God and offer up our prayers together, we find ourselves bound together with cords of heavenly love. Paul said that Christ came to make His people into "one new man" through Christ's death on the cross, and "through him we both have access by one Spirit unto the Father" (Eph. 2:15, 18). Thus, when we pray together with other believers in Christ, we experience our oneness in the Holy Spirit as children of one Father.

Christians often say to each other, "I'll pray for you." Why not say, "Let's pray together right now"? Few things comfort the heart as powerfully as listening to your friend cry out to your God to obtain grace for you in your time of need. Don't be intimidated about praying out loud. It does not need to be a long, theologically eloquent prayer, just a sincere prayer offered with love for a friend and with faith in Jesus Christ. Sometimes a simple, "Gracious heavenly Father, please be near to my friend and help her because she's really hurting," is all that it is needed.

---

50. Black, *Friendship,* 47.

The best of friends pray for each other and with each other. They are traveling companions on pilgrimage to the Celestial City. What Richard Baxter said of a godly spouse applies to Christian friendship in general:

> It is a mercy to have so near a friend to be a helper to your soul; to join with you in prayer and other holy exercises; to watch over you and tell you of your sins and dangers, and to stir up in you the grace of God, and remember [remind] you of the life to come, and cheerfully accompany you in the ways of holiness.[51]

9. *Repent together*. True friends are honest with each other. We all still sin. We all need correction. Will you be the kind of faithful friends who tell each other the truth when it hurts? This is a test of faithful friendship. Proverbs 27:5–6 says, "Open rebuke is better than secret love. Faithful are the wounds of a friend; but the kisses of an enemy are deceitful."

You may fear losing your friend, but if you speak in love and your friend is humble and loves the truth, then you can expect that words of correction will strengthen your relationship. Proverbs 28:23 says, "He that rebuketh a man afterwards shall find more favour than he that flattereth with the tongue." Learn to speak up, but also learn to shut up. Don't be like a repeated drip of water with constant

---

51. Baxter, *Christian Directory*, in *Practical Works*, 1:404.

criticisms. That kind of arrogance and insensitivity harms relationships.

Use what is called the sandwich principle when you want to constructively criticize a friend. You can learn from studying the apostle Paul's approach in his epistles, many of which are written to correct and instruct his friends. Did you ever notice that Paul often both opened and closed his epistles with words of thanksgiving to God and to his friends for the gracious qualities he saw in them? These are like the two slices of bread in a sandwich. Between these opening and closing comments, Paul inserts his "meat" of constructive criticism. Encourage your friends and tell them specific qualities God has worked in them for which you give thanks, and they will be more open to rebuke and correction when they feel love from you and can see that you are not condemning them as persons.

Biblical balance in our talk calls for both revealing sin and displaying grace. We need to speak both law and gospel to each other. Robert Kelleman says that true spiritual friends "are like the Puritans who practiced the art of loading the conscience with guilt. Like them, we know that to break the habitual web of sin's deceit, people need to experience the horrors of their sin against God and others." At the same time, such friends must be skilled in "the art of lightening the conscience with grace," for, "forgiveness by grace is the dynamic God uses not only to cleanse our lives, but also to change our love. Christ woos us back to God by grace."[52]

We often sin against each other. Strange as it may seem, the worst eruptions of our remaining corruption are often against those closest and dearest to us. Friendship between sinners can be preserved only by the hard work of reconciliation. Don't let the problem get out of hand. Proverbs 18:19 says, "A brother offended is harder to be won than a strong city: and their contentions are like the bars of a castle." Be quick to make peace, and be willing to admit your wrongdoings, repent of them, and make restitution. In the end, your relationship can become stronger than ever when both parties are willing to walk in humility and grace.

10. *Hope together*. In John Bunyan's allegory of the Christian life, *The Pilgrim's Progress*, one of Christian's best friends was named Faithful. Yet after Faithful died a martyr at Vanity Fair, God gave Christian another friend to accompany him on his pilgrimage. In fact, that friend stood with Christian to his dying days. His name was Hopeful, and he played a key role in upholding Christian's hope in his trials. Are you someone's "Hopeful"?

---

52. Robert W. Kellemen, *Spiritual Friends: A Methodology of Soul Care and Spiritual Direction*, rev. ed. (Winona Lake, Ind.: BMH Books, 2007), 52.

One of the blessings of Christian friendship is to encourage each other to keep our eyes fixed on Jesus and the coming of His kingdom. After Paul described what Christ's coming will mean for believers, he wrote, "Comfort one another with these words" (1 Thess. 4:18). Whether we are old or young, healthy or diagnosed with a terminal illness, we all need to be reminded that this world is not our home, but we have a place in the Father's house. We are to be "exhorting one another: and so much the more, as ye see the day approaching" (Heb. 10:25). Hope gives us patience, perseverance, and joy.

The more you use your Christian friendships to build up each other's hope in Christ, the closer you will become to each other. Hope unifies Christians (Eph. 4:4). What are our cultural, ethnic, and personal differences compared to the glorious kingdom we will share? All nations will hope in Christ, and it is this hope that enables us to glorify God with one mind and one mouth in all our diversity (Rom. 15:4–13).

Our hope transcends all earthly friendships, and so friendships should point us to our ultimate hope. When Andrew Fuller lay dying in April 1815, he was asked if he wanted to see John Ryland, who, as we have noted, was his oldest living friend. His response was terse and to the point: "He can do me no good." His reply seems to be an odd statement, lacking in appreciation for what their long friendship had meant to the two men. But it needs to be understood in context. In his final letter to Ryland, Fuller began by saying: "We have enjoyed much together, which I hope will prove an earnest of greater enjoyment in another world…. [There] I trust we shall meet, and part no more." Clearly, his feelings about his friendship with Ryland had undergone no alteration whatsoever. In the light of his impending death, however, there was only one friendship he knew to be needful in that moment: his friendship with the triune God—Father, Son, and Holy Spirit. As another eighteenth-century writer, James Newton, had written when faced with the death of his brother: "If we have God for our Friend, what need we to fear, Nothing, but without his Friendship we may be looked on as the most miserable of Men."[53]

CONCLUSION

So why is friendship important? This rapid survey of Scripture and church history reveals that it is a vital way that God works in the lives of His children to help them grow in grace and stay true to Christ. In this world, which is no friend to grace, God has designed the Christian life to be "a life together" in which believing friends aid one another and bear one another's burdens and pray for one another and encourage one another.[54] May God give us such

---

53. Diary entry for January 2, 1759, in *The Deserted Village. The Diary of an Oxfordshire Rector: James Newton of Nuneham Courtenay 1736–86*, transcribed and ed. Gavin Hannah (Dover, N.H.: Alan Sutton, 1992), 2.

54. Consider the "one another" passages in the New Testament as concrete ways in which we live out our Christian friendships; see, for

friendships—those that are deep, transparent, and affirming, and in which we serve as guardians of each other's souls.

Put into practice the practical guidelines to cultivate Christian friendship. Consider these ten ways of building a friendship to be the strands of a rope. The more areas of togetherness that you share with a friend, generally the stronger the bond of your friendship. Which strands are already in your friendship? Which ones can you start weaving into your relationship to make it stronger and more glorifying to God?

Don't expect too much of friendship. Don't expect perfect friends in this world; David Watson said, "Genuine fellowship comes when Christians stop relating to one another as righteous saints and accept one another as unrighteous sinners."[55] On the other hand, do seek good, real, and deep friendship—with patience, remembering what Thomas Watson said: "As the communion of saints is in our creed, so it should be in our company."[56] Seeking to build genuine, intimate fellowship takes time. Rushing into intimacy creates only false intimacy, often at the price of violating the boundaries of God's holy law. Patience in friendship and waiting on the Lord helps us to avoid twisting His gift of friends into occasions for sexual

instance, Romans 12:10; 15:5–7, 14; 16:16; Galatians 6:2; Ephesians 4:32; and James 5:16.

55. Quoted in John Blanchard, comp., *The Complete Gathered Gold* (Darlington, U.K.: Evangelical Press, 2006), 214.

56. Quoted in Blanchard, *Complete Gathered Gold*, 215.

immorality or homosexuality. Remember to "put ye on the Lord Jesus Christ, and make not provision for the flesh, to fulfil the lusts thereof" (Rom. 13:14). Even in the best of friendships, Christians remain pilgrims on their way to heaven. We pass through the night of this world, waiting for the coming dawn of the day of glory. Then we will experience a greater number, depth, intensity, and purity of friendships than we have dreamed of in this fallen world.

And there in heaven, Jesus Christ will be our very best Friend in perfection! Our friendship with Him will be rich and full and sin-free and utopian—forever! We cannot expect too much of His friendship in that glorious day when He will usher us into His and our eternal home to be with Him forever. Not only will He continue to treat us perfectly, but also we will finally treat Him perfectly—which is what we have always wanted to be able to do from the time we were first brought into a saving relationship with Him. Oh, to bask forever in His smile, feast in His presence, and commune with Him heart to heart, no longer having to know Him only as "through a glass darkly," but at last face-to-face! Hasten the day, Lord Jesus, when this mortal shall put on immortality, and this corruption, incorruption, and we shall ever be with our elder Brother, our glorious and perfect Friend, who truly sticks closer to us than any brother here on earth.